Contents

Preparing tools

This recipe book has lots
of cooking ideas.

What tools do we use...?

In the kitchen

Vic Parker

Heinemann LIBRARY

Little Nippers

www.heinemann.co.uk/library
Visit our website to find out more information about **Heinemann Library** books.

To order:
☎ Phone 44 (0) 1865 888066
▤ Send a fax to 44 (0) 1865 314091
▢ Visit the Heinemann Bookshop at www.heinemann.co.uk/library to browse our catalogue and order online.

First published in Great Britain by Heinemann Library, Halley Court, Jordan Hill, Oxford OX2 8EJ, part of Harcourt Education.
Heinemann is a registered trademark of Harcourt Education Ltd.

Editorial: Jilly Attwood and Louise Galpine
Design: Jo Hinton-Malivoire and bigtop, Bicester, UK
Models made by: Jo Brooker
Picture Research: Rosie Garai
Production: Séverine Ribierre

Originated by Dot Gradations
Printed and bound in China by South China Printing Company

ISBN 0 431 17153 X (hardback)
07 06 05 04 03
10 9 8 7 6 5 4 3 2 1

ISBN 0 431 17158 0 (paperback)
07 06 05 04 03
10 9 8 7 6 5 4 3 2 1

British Library Cataloguing in Publication Data
Parker, Vic
What tools do we use ...? In the kitchen
643.3
A full catalogue record for this book is available from the British Library.

Acknowledgements
The publishers would like to thank the following for permission to reproduce photographs:
Gareth Boden pp. **4, 5, 6, 7, 8, 9, 10, 11, 12, 13, 14, 15, 16, 17, 18/19, 20, 21, 22, 23.**

Cover photograph reproduced with permission of Gareth Boden.

The publishers would like to thank Annie Davy for her assistance in the preparation of this book.

Every effort has been made to contact copyright holders of any material reproduced in this book. Any omissions will be rectified in subsequent printings if notice is given to the publishers.

2

One of these tools is for peeling potatoes.

Which one is it?

5

Slicing tools

Knives are very sharp - be careful of your fingers.

Chop!

Chop!

Chop!

This pizza cutter will slice up pizza safely.

Mixing tools

What a **gooey** mixture you can make with a whisk!

Watch it whirr round and round.

Mashing tools

You can have a smashing time with a pestle and mortar.

Crash!

Bash!

Mash!

Squeezing tools

This juicer is easy peasy lemon squeezy!

12

What is being **squeezed** out of this machine?

It's **long,** thin spaghetti!

Sprinkling tools

salt shaker

pepper shaker

Icing sugar is sprinkling through this sieve like snow.

15

Cooking tools

A saucepan is deep.

A frying pan is flat.

A wok is flat too.

A wooden spoon is for stirring round and round.

A fish slice is for flipping over.

17

Baking tools

Have you ever baked biscuits?

There are lots of biscuit cutters to choose from.

19

Tidying up tools

Lots of tools to wash up!

What are these kitchen tools?

colander

measuring jug

wok

masher

fish slice

wooden spoon

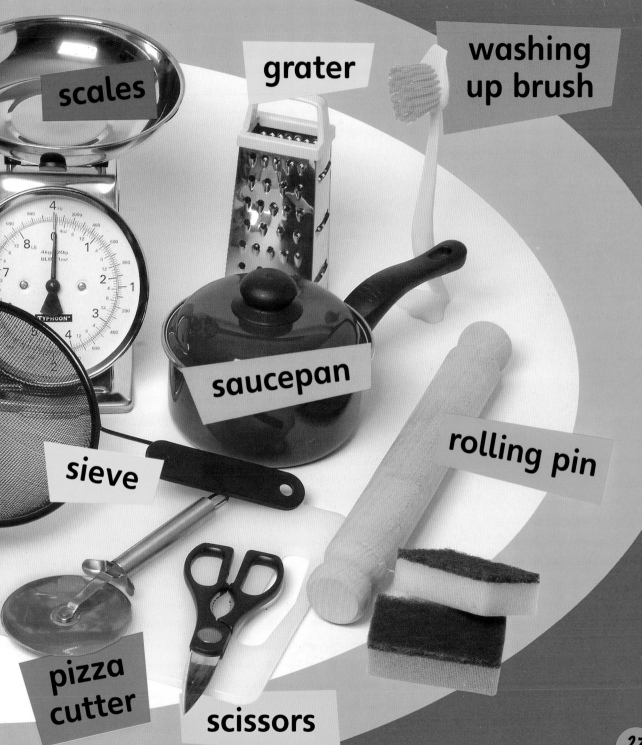

scales

grater

washing up brush

saucepan

rolling pin

sieve

pizza cutter

scissors

23

Index

The end

Notes for adults

'What tools do we use . . .?' explores a variety of tools that a young child may come across in different situations. The series encourages young children to think creatively about the different jobs these tools do, and what other tools they might use to do the same job. The books provide opportunities for discussing how the tools should be used safely and correctly, and what materials the tools are made from. There are four titles in the series: *At school, At home, In the kitchen,* and *In the garden.* Used together, the books will enable comparison of similarities and differences between a wide variety of tools.

The key curriculum Early Learning Goals relevant to this series are:
• learn skills by using a range of tools
• select tools and techniques necessary to shape, assemble and join a range of materials
• talk about tools and their effects and how they work
• realize that tools can be used for a purpose and introduce children to appropriate tools to work on different materials
• encourage children to use the correct names for tools.

This book introduces the reader to a range of tools they may use in the kitchen. The book will help children extend their vocabulary, as they will hear new words such as *recipe,* and *pestle* and *mortar.* You may like to introduce and explain other new words yourself, such as *weighing scales* and *measuring jug.*

Additional information about tools
A tool is defined as any object which you use to perform an operation to achieve an end. Tools can be small, like pencils, or large, like lawn mowers. Tools can be hand-held, such as screwdrivers, or stationary, such as pasta-making machines. Tools can be manual, like saws, or power-driven, such as hair-dryers. Tools can be classified by their function, such as: joining things or shaping things; by their mode of operation, such as: sticking things or cleaning things; or by their mode of action, such as: tools that cut, tools that mix, tools that suck.

Follow-up activities
• Identify all the tools in the kitchen which are sharp and which need special care or adult supervision.
• Help your child fill a washing-up bowl with different kitchen tools, then cover it with a tea-towel and see how many your child can remember.